# 10 Ways to save and grow money

By:

Shana Trahan, M. Ed, LPC

Table of Contents

# Foreword

Forget the Joneses! You must focus on you and your family. You DON'T have 24 hours a day. After work you have 16 hours, after sleep, you ONLY have 8-10 hours left to create the kind of life you desire! Who are you? What do you possess and what are your short term and long-term goals? What is the best way to get there? Are their multiple routes? What is your why? The why is your reason for working smart and consistently to get where you are trying to go. Make those 8-10 hours count!

Without the foundational knowledge and understanding, how do you take your life to the next level? Your successful financial future and great quality of life depends on you learning and putting the things you learn into action. What are you waiting for? Read onward!

## Inspiring Quotes

"Though I have come through many trials, I won't be in denial. Each one has made me a better person."

-Shana Trahan

"I have not failed. I have just found 10,000 ways that don't work."

-Thomas A. Edison

"There is no perfect answer but there are always multiple solutions."

-Shana Trahan

"If we command our wealth, we shall be rich and free. If our wealth commands us, we are poor indeed".

-Edmund Burke

"Many folk think they aren't good at earning money, when what they don't know is how to use it."

-Frank A. Clark

"An investment in knowledge pays the best interest."

-Benjamin Franklin

"Formal education will make you a living; self-education will make you a fortune."

-Jim Rohn

"Empty pockets never held anyone back. Only empty heads and hearts can do that."

-Norman Vincent Peale

"Money is a terrible master but an excellent servant."

-P.T. Barnum

"Wealth is the ability to fully experience life."

-Henry David Thoreau

"It's not how much money you make, but how much you keep, how hard it works for you and how many generations you keep it for."

-Robert Kiyosaki

"As long as you're going to be thinking anyway, think big."

-Donald Trump

## Missed Opportunities

*Questions to ponder.....*

How do you view money?

_____

_____

_____

_____

Why do you see money that way?

_____

_____

_____

_____

What money lessons did you learn as a child, directly or

indirectly?

_____

_____

_____

_____

How much money do you earn from your salary?

Gross_____        Net _____

Amount from other sources? _____

What is keeping you from earning more?

_____

_____

_____

_____

While growing up, what missed opportunities did you have

as it relates to lessons you could have been taught about

money by adults who loved you?

_____

_____

_____

_____

_____

As a young child, many of us are shown what we would term as a piggy bank. Every now and again, our parents, grandparents, other relatives or friends would give us some change in jest. We'd delightfully take it, excitedly as if we'd just received a million tax free dollars to spend. Upon shaking it and hearing each coin hit the other, we were satisfied. This is the innocence of youth. 100% return and no investment, a sweet deal.

Unfortunately, for many children, this is the beginning and the end of lessons about money. For some of us, the opportunity to go with our parents to this huge building with people standing behind windows seemed interesting. As a child, the fondest memory of this place was the lollipops they would give each child after a transaction. As a child, most of us never knew why we were there, what was going on and why our parents were talking to the strangers behind the windows at the "bank".

Unbeknownst to us, their parents hadn't shown them any tricks to the trade of money. Reflecting back on the many times of playing the Monopoly game, probably because the people I played with didn't know-we just looked at it as a game. We never looked at is as an opportunity for the future. We never looked at the strategies we used to buy low and sell high as something that could be used in real life. We never associated the luxury tax to real life and how we are made to pay taxes in the U.S. We didn't even know what taxes were and how they affected our lives.

Another game that was taken for granted was The Game of Life. It was clearly spelled out in the name, but it was more like a fairy tale than real world experiences. While some children had more grown up life experiences and probably understood that the game was about real living and functioning in the world, I imagine that most children didn't.

For the plethora of us who have been in church with our parents and have observed them putting money into the collection plate or even being on the receiving end of money so that we could put it into the collection plate in children's church-they had yet another missed opportunity.

Dad or mom was sitting at the table counting out the money earned from his or her job and trying to figure out which bills to pay or not to pay. As children, of course we just kept running around playing-I was probably combing the hair on my Barbie head, the one with the shoulders. You would have imagined that I would have grown into a stylist considering all the time I put into wetting, combing, styling and pinning up her hair. Remember that Barbie head?

We can all think back to missed opportunities in various areas of our lives. The question is, "Is it possible to recapture what we missed or is it best to learn from our mistakes and the mistakes of others?"

If you have breath flowing through your body, you have an opportunity to learn, correct faux pas and to just do better.

Let's go back to the game of Monopoly. What are 6 lessons you can learn from it and teach your offspring?

## Monopoly Lessons

1. Things must be done decently and in order
2. Obtaining money and growing it is important
3. You can grow money using real estate and utilities
4. Taxes can help or hurt you
5. Everything costs and quality costs more
6. Everyone won't have the same outcome
7. In life you can win or lose
8. You must invest slow and steady
9. You must invest strategically

10. Invest in properties within the same community or general area

So, I was always in the grocery store with my mother or grandmother. There were hundreds of pricing signs around the markets. There, many signs displayed cost per pound, cost per ounce and total costs.

Unfortunately, I was never taught about these things through my experiences in the grocery store. I learned about these things in math class. Being that I was in the store weekly, it would seem to me that someone would have shared how all these things worked, and how they related to a person's earnings from their career. No such thing ever happened.

Since I know better now, I teach my 5-year-old granddaughter these lessons while we are in various stores. She's inquisitive and she wants to know the fine details. With a memory like an elephant, she remembers and even reminds me of some of the things I have taught her during subsequent visits.

So, I'm not blaming my parents for their lack of insight into how they could have prepared me and my siblings better when we were younger. My emphasis is to you as a parent, aunt, uncle or any relative that a young person spends time with, make every moment a time to build your relationship and an opportunity to teach them positive and useful lessons about money that will last for a lifetime.

What will you do to ensure that you don't allow for missed opportunities for your children or children around you?

_____

_____

_____

_____

_____

_____

_____

# Chapter Two

## *Eat Less and Exercise More*

*More questions to ponder….*

What does how much you eat have to do with money?

_____

_____

_____

Do you prefer a greater quantity of food or a greater

quality? _____

Do you exercise your mind, body or your eating utensils

more? _____

Why?_____

_____

_____

You are wondering what this has to do with money. Food has everything to do with money. It has to do with how we use our time. Of course, it's not expected that a person will perform or produce like a robot. How you utilize your available time matters. Think about it. We have 24 hours in a day.

## Below Average Producer

| Priority | Activity | Time Used in Hours |
|----------|----------|--------------------|
| 1 | Sleep | 10 |
| 2 | Eat | 3-4 |
| 5 | Family Time | 1 |
| 3 | Work | 8 |
| 6 | Research/Reading | 0 |
| 4 | Traveling back and forth | 2 |
| 7 | Exercise | 0 |

## Average Producer

| Priority | Activity | Time Used In Hours |
|---|---|---|
| 1 | Sleep | 8 |
| 2 | Eat | 1.5 |
| 5 | Family Time | 2.5 |
| 3 | Work | 8.5 |
| 6 | Research/Reading | 1 or less |
| 4 | Traveling back and forth | 2.0 |
| 7 | Exercise | 30 minutes |

What things do you see on this chart that are representative of what you do?

_____

_____

_____

## Above Average Producer

| Priority | Activity | Time Used in Hours |
|----------|----------|--------------------|
| 3 | Sleep | 6 |
| 6 | Eat | 1 |
| 4 | Family Time | 4 |
| 5 | Work | 7 |
| 1 | Research/ Reading | 3 |
| 7 | Traveling back and forth | 1 |
| 2 | Exercise | 2 |

What do you make of these charts?

_____

_____

Which chart most accurately represents you?

_____

Based upon the chart that most accurately represents your life do you agree that you are living below average, average or above average life? Yes or No

Why don't you make your own chart?

**My current life:**

| Priority | Activity | Time Used in Hours |
|----------|----------|--------------------|
|          | Sleep    |                    |
|          | Eat      |                    |
|          | Family Time |                 |
|          | Work     |                    |
|          | Research/Reading |             |
|          | Traveling back and forth |     |
|          | Exercise |                    |

Is your current life utilization getting you what you want? Yes or No   What changes might you need to make to ensure a better outcome for the life you want for you

and your family?

_____

_____

_____

_____

_____

When will you be willing to make the changes?

| Change | Change by date |
|--------|----------------|
|        |                |
|        |                |
|        |                |
|        |                |
|        |                |
|        |                |
|        |                |

## My projected life:

| Priority | Activity | Time Used in Hours |
|---|---|---|
| | Sleep | |
| | Eat | |
| | Family Time | |
| | Work | |
| | Research/Reading | |
| | Traveling back and forth | |
| | Exercise | |

Let's get back to eating. When we eat higher quality foods, in less quantity than lower quality foods, we gain more energy. When we exercise more, we gain more energy. When we read, we think, and we burn more calories. We need less sleep because we eat healthier, exercise more and burn more energy and clear our minds which causes our hours of productivity to be increased.

In no way, shape or form am I suggesting that you rush through your eating. I am saying that when things are prioritized in a way that is beneficial to you that you get more done. Does that make sense to you?

---

I know some people who are "Foodies" and they spend more time eating than the law allows. This is mainly because the "Foodie" experience is about taking time to savor the food mixed with a bit of socializing. What if they enjoyed good food but didn't make it a priority between 1 and 3? I was watching a detailed video that talked about how people don't have to eat every day. It also discussed how the food pyramid keeps people gaining weight. Weight maintenance can be achieved by monitoring calories, water intake and regularly exercising. **Lesson**: Just because something is generally accepted doesn't make it the best fit for everyone.

# Chapter Three

BUDGET

*The*

*Mysterious Budget*

*More questions to ponder….*

<u>True or False</u>

- Money is best under my mattress. ____

- I should just spend until my money is gone. _____

- 80% of my money should go to my housing. ____

- My budget includes my investments. _____

- I should show my children how I create a budget. __

- A budget should change monthly. ____

- My travel expenses should be budgeted. __

- A budget should be run in the red. ___

See the answers at the end of the chapter.

What is a budget? A budget is an established plan of how you will save, pay your bills and invest. How does having a budget save you money? Having a budget saves you money because you are better able to track your income, outgoing, savings and investments. If you don't track your spending, it's probable that you will end up with more month and not enough money to cover the expenditures.

So, where should you begin to figure out budgeting? Some people have written a budget out on a napkin, on the back of a bill, on a blank sheet of paper and even on a paper grocery bag. Nowadays, there are many sites, apps and templates that you can use. Sometimes, it's good to look at others and decide which parts you need and what you need to add to yours.

**Some areas you should consider when budgeting:**

- ☐ Housing
- ☐ Healthcare
- ☐ Food (groceries/eating out)
- ☐ Insurance (auto, home)
- ☐ Transportation (note, gas, repairs)
- ☐ Savings/Investments
- ☐ Debt (student loans, credit cards)
- ☐ Clothing (purchases, dry cleaning, repair)
- ☐ Entertainment (activities that cost)
- ☐ Emergency Fund (2-3x monthly income)

Housing can be broken down into rent/mortgage, light bill, gas bill, water bill, garbage collection and items such as those. So, it could be as detailed as you'd like.

Healthcare can be broken down into deductibles, medication, parking costs as well as actual insurance coverage costs if it's paid monthly, post tax.

Your budget should be broken down on a monthly basis while taking into consideration the days you get paid and how much your net income is.

Via etsy.com via pinterest (pic)

This is one example. Inside of your computer lives budgeting tools as well. You can also access multiple sites such as:

- Kiplinger-Household Budget Worksheet
- https://www.kiplinger.com/tool/spending/T007-S001-budgeting-worksheet-a-household-budget-for-today-a/index.php
- NerdWallet Budget
- https://www.nerdwallet.com/blog/finance/budget-worksheet/
- Dave Ramsey Budget
- https://www.daveramsey.com/budgeting/how-to-budget
- Another Budgeting Tool
- https://www.everydollar.com/?gclid=Cj0KCQiA_s7f BRDrARIsAGEvF8TYeV4S8Dkgnhk0uXYel_cM7aSpxq XOaOmSSOthl8Hdz7Raxzy8GzIaAov5EALw_wcB
- Government Sample Budget

- https://www.consumer.gov/content/make-budget-worksheet

## Budgeting Apps

*NerdWallet

*Intuit Mint

*YNAB

*PocketGuard

*Prism

*Albert

## Budgeting strategies

A few strategies that have worked for me are the envelope system and zero based budgeting. While both were developed many years ago, Dave Ramsey also has a version of each that you can check out as well. Some people use the 50/30/20 budgeting.

In short, to use the envelope system you must create your budget first. Next you must label your envelopes. After that you must withdraw the funds from the bank to cover the exact amounts that must be in each envelope. You must determine how many of each denomination you will need including change, i.e. a bill is $26.75. You'll need to put the $.75 in the envelope with the $20, a $5, a $1 bill. All the expenses will be paid in cash.

A key in this plan is that you're not supposed to borrow or share money between envelopes. Remember, your budget will likely change monthly as bill costs change and some items are being paid down or have been paid off.

The zero-based system requires you to account for every cent of your earnings. If your net is $3,271.29, you must create a budget to include saving, entertainment and investing along with the other categories that doesn't leave you with a cent not being accounted for.

In 50/30/20 budgeting, you're supposed to divide expenditures into groups.

| 50% | Rent, gas, utilities (things you **NEED**) |
|-----|--------------------------------------------|

| 30% | Things you Want... |
|------|--------------------|
| 20% | Savings, debts, credit cards, investments |

In the end you'll have to decide which strategy works best for you. There is no one size fits all. Something that is vital is choosing a budget type that you believe you can stick with. If you try one and it doesn't work for you, try another. Refrain from being discouraged. Most families have different components, demographics and characteristics. The main point is to choose strategies for the success of your family and implement them.

*More questions to ponder....*

- Which budgeting strategy should I use first?

  _____

- Where are copies of all my bills so that I can record each including the name, address, amount owed, the date, amount paid and the means by which you pay it?

- _____

  _____

  _____

- Where can I find income statements and check stubs and a calculator to begin working on a budget? _____

## The answers to your true and false questions.

1. No, money should never be stored under the mattress when it can be earning more money.

2. If you spend until your money is gone, then, what will you have? You will have nothing.

3. You should spend about 30% of your gross or less on housing.

4.  Most budgets you see won't include investments, but it is important to plan for investing and to include it in your budget. The least amount you should be investing is 15% of your gross income.

5. Certainly, your budget should include travel and lodging if this is something that you plan to do.

6. A budget should not be run in the red. If your budget is being run into the red, you have several factors to consider.

- Are you living very close to or within the budgeting guidelines? _____

- Are you paying more than the minimum payment on debt that doesn't charge interest?

  _____

- Are you dining out more than cooking at home?

  _____

- Are you buying duplicates of items you already have at home when you already have enough to last you? _____

- Always check the cupboards before going shopping.

**Note:** Every budget model varies by a few percentage points, but don't focus on that.

# Budgeting Guidelines
for the cost of living by category

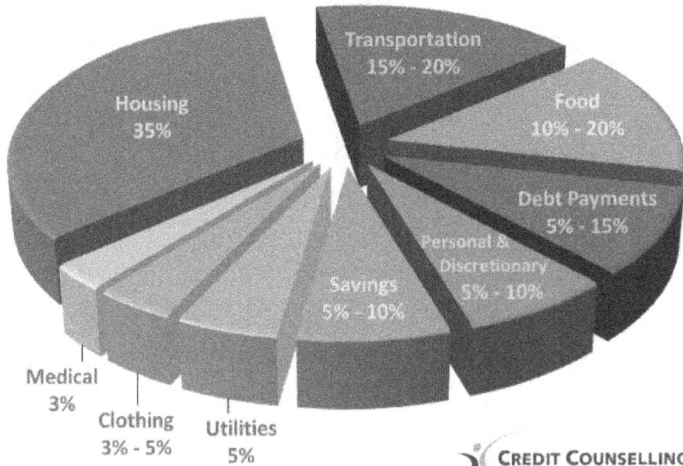

Transportation
15% - 20%

Food
10% - 20%

Housing
35%

Debt Payments
5% - 15%

Personal &
Discretionary
5% - 10%

Savings
5% - 10%

Medical
3%

Clothing
3% - 5%

Utilities
5%

CREDIT COUNSELLING
SOCIETY

If you already know the inside and out about budgeting or once you have learned, that would be a great time and opportunity to teach your children.

# Chapter

# Four

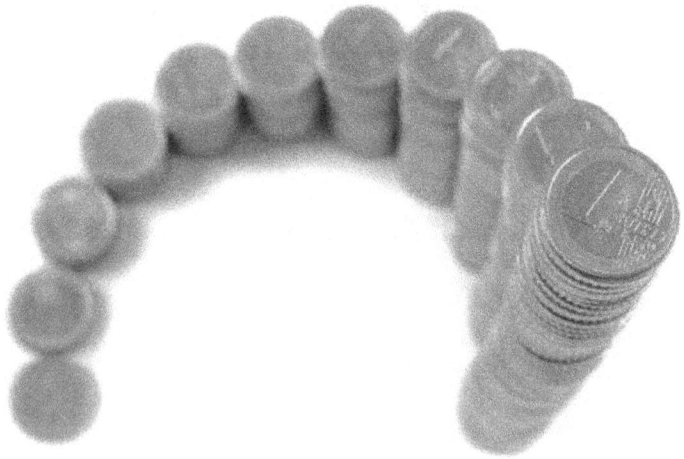

Spare Change

What is spare change? It's the coins in the bottom of a purse, in a piggy bank, in an unused ashtray, under the sofa pillows, in the five gallon water bottle and what you get in your hand a the store when you give the clerk more than you owed her. I have saved coins but never as fanatically as some people I know. It's good to save and it's always good to have some cash on hand. I learned that with Hurricane Katrina when I wasn't able to access some atm's and banks that were only in that region, after the storm.

Now there are apps that help you to save and invest your spare change. You will have to read the specifics of each. In each app you can choose multiple settings that help you to save your spare change and more. Check out: www.acorns.com , www.qapital.com ,

https://digit.co/ , Chime is in the Google Play Store and in iTunes, https://www.longgame.co/ ,

and https://claritymoney.com/ .

**According to Acorns it enables you to:**

1. Invest automatically

2. Set aside spare change or extra cash as you go about your day with Roundups and Recurring Investments.

3. Get the easiest IRA, Acorns Later, and save for retirement without thinking about it

4. Sit back and let your money grow over time in diversified portfolios constructed by experts.

**According to Qapital, it enables you to partake in:**

1. Money Missions are fun challenges that help you think a bit deeper about your spending. You'll unlock helpful insights into how you use your money now so you can use it better in the future.

2. Use our Payday Divvy to define your spending, rather than letting it define you. Divvy up significant deposits in a few taps to make sure you cover your commitments while funding your future.

3. A Qapital account opens lots of powerful ways to work with your money, and to make your money work harder. Find your Spending Sweet Spot and achieve the perfect balance between what you want now, and what you want most.

4. Qapital's pre-built portfolios are ideal for budding investors – give us a timeline and amount and we'll do the rest. We'll even diversify your funds, so you don't have all your eggs in one basket.

5. Saving 'just because' is fine but saving for something special is fun. Qapital helps you get there faster with Goals and Rules – two clever ways to supercharge your saving with little effort. Plus, you can even team up with others to reach joint goals.

**According to digit you can access:**

1. Automated saving-app knows when to save

2. Unlimited goals

3. 1% Savings Bonus

4. Pay down credit card debt

5. Unlimited withdrawals

6. Low Balance Protection

7. No account minimums

8. Overdraft Reimbursement

**According to NerdWallet, Chime:**

1. "Chime is a mobile-only bank, so it's not like your traditional neighborhood branch. But it still has all the fundamentals and, with FDIC insurance, it's a safe place to keep your money. It has a "spending" account, as well as a savings account. When you buy something with your bank card, you can have Chime round up the amount to the nearest dollar and deposit the difference in savings. Chime has no monthly fees or overdraft fees, but its interest rate is low. Checks and cash can be difficult to deposit."

## According to Longgame:

1. It's FDIC insured and earns interest, plus get rewards as you achieve your goals.

2. Play fun mobile games. The more you save the more chances you earn to play.

3. Win prizes up to $1,000,000, or win cryptocurrencies like Bitcoin and Ether.

4. Earn interest and withdraw at any time.

5. Achieve your financial goals with rewards that keep you encouraged and on the right path.

## According to Clarity Money:

1. With a Marcus online savings account, we help you save towards a goal

2. Helps to cancel subscriptions

3. Analyze your spending and income to find cards that might interest you

4. Can help you stay under budget by clearly displaying your finances and showing when you overspend

So, there you go folks, plenty of savings and investment, and earning possibilities-even with crypto and bitcoin. So, don't let your spare change sit in a drawer, put it to good use in one of these apps. Go to each app site and get as much information as you can. Write out your list of pro's and con's and decide what you will do.

- What are your financial goals? Which tools do you believe would work best for you?

_____

_____

_____

After you've hidden a 30-day emergency stash in your home, everything else should be invested. Your in-home stash shouldn't be under the mattress. No friends or family should be aware of your stash and its location. Never tell anyone that you have cash in your home. There are many creative places to put it: In a sock inside a sock drawer, in a tampon box, in an opaque cookie jar, in an old book, in an envelope and plastic bag inside of your attic door or behind your washing machine. These aren't all the places to stash your 30-day emergency fund but do put it away.

Your emergency cash that is 3-6 months of your income should be working in a money market or an interest-bearing savings. Check NerdWallet for the best interest rates for each. Some of the apps allow you to withdraw funds in 3-7 days as well. If you choose to use an app to save with since you'll have that 30-day stash on hand, that could prove more beneficial. If you find a money market, checking or savings account that pays more than 3%, one of those might be a consideration.

So, what is emergency cash? Emergency cash is not for the things we want. It's for the things we need. It's there for a layoff, major systems failing in your home, a deductible after a major flood or storm or even a hospital deductible for unexpected medical concerns. It's not for that last-minute trip your friend invited you to. That isn't an exhaustive list of what the emergency funds or for, but hopefully it causes you to understand when those funds should be used.

What does an emergency fund consist of? Think about what it takes to run your household for 1 month, every aspect of your home. For example: Rent, transportation costs, utility bills, childcare, food, savings, personal care (and other things that are in your personal budget). Take that monthly total and multiply it by 3 or 6.

If your household budget is $2,200, then, for a 3-month emergency fund you'll need to have $6600 saved and for a 6-month emergency fund, you'd need to have $13,200 in savings or local investments like the ones described above. So, now is the opportune time to research for opportunities to invest while saving to put your family in a secure position in the event of any emergency.

## Take Pause

Think back on all the things that you have read so far. What are the top 3 things that you feel will most impact your future?

_____

_____

_____

Who will you choose as an accountability partner to ensure that you follow through on these things?

_____

_____

Is there anything stopping you from moving forward in any of the areas listed? _____

If no, great! If so, what are they and how are they stopping you from making your goals materialize?

_____

_____

_____

_____

_____

Who can you reach out to for clarity?

_____

_____

What do they know about this topic?

_____

_____

_____

# Chapter 5

## Stuck on name brands

Is name brand required or will No Name, also known as the
less advertised brand work sometimes? Certainly, while
finding your place in the world, you want to, "Borrowing

from the Migos again", "Walk it like I talk it". You want to get some nice shoes, a nice suit and a nice watch, earrings and a necklace until you've been able to get to your financially secure place.

One smart person I knew many years ago had the income to buy loads of clothes. Instead she had a few suit jackets (blue and black) a few skirts (blue and black), a few pairs of pants (blue and black) and of course a few pairs of shoes (blue and black) two pairs of high heels and two pairs of flats. She rotated these things until she couldn't wear them anymore.

In a school where I worked, I bought uniforms for myself that was the same as the uniforms the students wore. While I was an excellent model of how the students should be wearing their uniforms, I also saved loads of cash. I didn't feel as if I had to out dress anyone else. I felt confident that I was doing something worthwhile.

The students loved that I dressed like them and my wallet enjoyed the fact that I wasn't in the mall splurging.

So, did I wear designer khaki pants? For me, as a shopper I look at style, quality of fabric and fit. If it happens to be a brand that people are familiar with, then so be it.

If designer things are in your budget and you're still able to save and invest between 15 to 22% of your gross income, have at it. If you haven't been investing this much, perhaps it's time to rethink your strategy. Some of the people who are most money smart shop at resale shops, garage sales and Goodwill or Salvation Army shops for clothing or even at Macy's One Day Sales where you can often buy new items for pennies on the dollar. Nowadays, people are selling all sorts of clothing and household items on apps and many sites at a cost lower than you would find in the store. You can even find band names that you love.

Don't forget that the major retailers watch the same runway shows in New York, Paris, Milan and Hong Kong. The truth is other shops will have items that look very much like the high-priced designer items that you love.

So, this also spans into groceries. Read the labels. Do they have the same ingredients? If one can of early peas costs $.79 per can and other costs $1.29 per can and it has a name you've heard of before on it, does that mean that you should pay the $1.29?

Another thing to consider instead of drink mixes is adding fresh citrus fruit, cucumber or fresh mint to water in the refrigerator.

**Term:** Frugal-highly considerate of expenditures

**Tip:** Surmise your purchases large and small before you make them. Of course, your budget which should be based upon your income should guide you.

# Chapter 6

## Couponing

I remember being a young child trifling through the Sunday newspaper looking for the funnies and noticing the coupons. I pondered them for years. I am still learning about coupons. You have certainly heard of people shopping with coupons and only having to pay pennies for a basket full of items. Initially this seems like a daunting task; one that is unreal.

Many people ask if couponing is worth it. Using one coupon by itself usually isn't a savings nor is it noteworthy. Historically, the coupons offered would be for one of the highest priced items in that category. So, if you got a coupon for A-1 Steak sauce, (the best tasting in my opinion), while you might get $.25 off, you'd still be paying more for that bottle than other brands. With one coupon per item, you're usually spending more on your cart of groceries.

Have you ever used coupons? If so, what's been your experience? _____

_____

Have you ever heard of extreme couponing? _____

Do you think learning how to effectively use couponing can help you to save and grow your money?

_____

Circle the supplies that you have: computer, cell phone, printer, the ability to order a Sunday paper (the main one with coupons), access to internet services and the ability to add, subtract and multiply or a calculator.

Those are all the things you need to start your journey. Couponing has gotten so popular that people have begun to dedicate rooms to all the items they're able to get for free or nearly free on their couponing journeys.

*Step 1:* Research and read the store policies for the stores that you visit for the bulk of your shopping such as: Walgreens, CVS, Walmart, HEB, Target, Sav A Lot, etc. Often the cashier won't know the policy and will attempt to deny you the use of multiple coupons because they don't know the policy. You might have to ask for a manager.

*Step 2:* Copy and paste those policies or rewrite them so that you can clearly understand what you can and can't do at each establishment.

*Step 3:* Look up The Krazy Coupon Lady to get some of her expert tips and subscribe to her feed.

*Step 4:* Get a binder, folder or some type of coupon keeping system that will enable you to keep track of your coupons and be able to access them quickly (at home or in the store).

*Step 5:* Decide upon your menu for the week as well as consider personal care needs and household needs (toothpaste, Tide laundry detergent, etc..).

*Step 6:* Check your cupboards and cabinets to see what you need for the upcoming week.

*Step 7:* Make your grocery list.

*Step 8:* Check for corresponding coupons on items that you need for this week as well as for coupons or store deals for things that you use regularly in the household.

*Step 9:* Sit down and do some math to determine which deals will save you the most and allow you to get the best bang for your buck.

Note: If you end up with a lot of extra things, you may save them to use later. Some couponers sell some extras to friends and neighbors for a fair market value slightly

marked down from the usual store purchase price.

*Step 10:* Go shopping

Please look for additional resources in the resource section

in the rear of the book.

# Chapter 7

## Growing Money

Does money sitting in your wallet grow? How can you grow money? Is it possible to put it in the bottom of a flowerpot under some soil, to water it and to grow coins and dollars? Of course not, but sometimes the process is similar. In other words, there are some buy and hold method of investing and saving that works.

Growing money is something unique to each party because each person has a different set of interests, skills and the available amount of time to put effort towards that growth.

For example, one person might love automobiles and choose to obtain a licensed reseller permit so that he or she could purchase automobiles from auctions to sell to people who want cars, at a profit. If you have no interest in cars, fixing cars, don't know anyone who could repair them cheaply, you wouldn't want to undertake this type of way to grow money.

Other people are crafty or creative and perhaps makes or designs things. This person could certainly attend craft shows and perhaps school and community carnivals as well as selling on a site such as ETSY.

Before I get deeper into this, you must assess your situation and make some solid choices.

How much money do you have to invest or grow?

Weekly_____ Monthly_____

This amount should be determined after you have established a viable budget and these funds can't come from money that is required for you to meet your basic needs or your emergency fund money. This money should be money you have after you have paid off credit card debts and other interest-bearing debt.

How much time do you have available to manage the growth of this money? Weekly _____ Monthly___ What type of risk are you willing to take? For the sake of this book, will consider three types of risk: Low, moderate or high. When you take a low risk, your investment is more stable and has a chance of growing. The growth of a low risk investment is usually much slower and the amount of growth is usually much smaller than the returns on something considered moderate or high risk. The higher the risk, the higher potential of the return. Moderate risk would usually have a higher and faster rate of return than a low risk investment. Moving to a moderate risk would also mean that your investment would possibly incur greater volatility (movement up and down with a greater potential for earnings or loss). If you were to lose a portion of your investment, would you be okay with that while the market or your particular investment rebuilds?

A high-risk investment will have the highest potential for growth and loss. Just like you can invest your $1,000,000, you can lose it and must rebuild. On the other hand, that

one million could turn into two or three million. So, which

type of investment are you most comfortable with?

_____

# Chapter 8

Your commitment

When it all boils down, it comes to whether you're willing to put in the work to make all the information you read come together. It's quite easy to buy a book. It's easy to carry it home and to place it on a shelf. It's easy to read the foreword and the back cover to determine if it has the potential to add to you as a person. The difficult part in any challenge that man takes on is choosing to be committed to the actual undertaking at hand.

Where are you in your commitment?

_____

_____

_____

Have you highlighted important parts of the text?

_____

Have you written down or begun to ponder how and when to begin to put some planning and actions into play to execute all that is required to see positive and fruitful results?

_____

_____

_____

Have you mentioned it to friends? _____

Have you determined who your accountability partner will be? _____

If so, does that person know that you've chosen them to be your partner? _____

Who is that person? _____

## Accountability

What does that look like? First, determine which goal you will begin with. Next, identify a person who you know will check in with you and encourage you toward your goal. This person should also be available to bounce ideas off as well. Think in terms of a friend who usually accomplishes what they set out to accomplish who might have 10 to 20 minutes per week for you as needed.

If for any reason you don't have anyone like that in your circle, reach out to someone in your company, other organizations you belong to, business owners in your neighborhood and if all else fails try a local church. If none of those work, try LinkedIn. If you reach out to someone on

LinkedIn: make sure they're in an industry of interest and that your profile is nice and professional. Be prepared, people who don't know you might be inclined to charge you for their time, for, with their time comes wisdom. It also ensures them that their time is important to you.

## Checklists

I am a checklist fan. You can use checklists to make sure that you get the tasks which are most important to you accomplished. Each night before you go to bed, consider the top 5 projects and what you'll need to accomplish to get them completed. Consider family goals as well, "Read Janie a bedtime story". This way, the most important things have a place in your schedule and get done. Many people complete 70% of their schedule or checklist daily. There are many factors that affect that outcome. Consider your daily schedule, the time you get up and go to bed. How much time is family time?

_____

During what time frame do you intend to complete the

checklist? _____

      How many and which activities will you be able to realistically accomplish in the time you've set aside for those activities?

_____

_____

_____

_____

_____

## Schedule

There are two schedules. There is the schedule you currently follow and the schedule you'd need to follow to get the things that you want to do. The type of schedule you will create will be based upon your values-the things you value as well as upon the goals you've set. So, while your exact schedule isn't known to me, the two schedules that will be displayed will give you an excellent example of how to go from a schedule of achieving less than you'd like to one of achievement.

Before we get to that, you'll have to define your values.

What are the most important things in your life?

_____

_____

_____

_____

_____

Now, put them (people, activities) in value order.

|  |
|--|
|  |
|  |
|  |
|  |

Think about these things/people you value, will these

things or people help or support you in making the goals

you hope to achieve? Are any of those things or people

interfering with you finding success in multiple areas? If so,

who or what are they? _____

_____

_____

_____

Are you willing to put those things or people to the side to

garner the success you'd like to have?

Yes or no? If you said no, it's your choice and that can

affect the outcome you may have alluded to wanting.

# Chapter 9

# Resources

Bloomberg : www.bloomberg.com

Money : www.money.com/money

Investopedia: www.investopedia.com

Finance: www.finance.yahoo.com/videos/

Entrepreneur: www.entrepreneur.com

Banking: www.thebalance.com

Money Market: www.investopedia.com

Please note that all resources were read, reviewed and active when this book was published. While these resources can be quite helpful during your journey, realize that you can certainly find opportunities all over the internet, in books on Amazon and on Kindle.

This book was written because of the lessons learned in the real life of a real person. Growing up poor and always admiring simple things like people having the ability to have nice clothes, a home of their own and being able to take vacations, sometimes multiple vacations and parents with cars created a desire in me to learn how to save and grow rich. I even had friends in high school with cars and I always wondered what the difference was between me and them. Have you ever thought about that or something comparable to that? If so, now you know the difference and you can apply what you learned here to your life and the lives of your children. Live and grow rich.

# Bibliography

https://www.investopedia.com/terms/z/zbb.asp

https://www.mvelopes.com/the-history-of-envelope-budgeting/

https://www.nerdwallet.com/blog/finance/budgeting-saving-tools/#nw-toc-heading-1

https://www.lendkey.com/blog/how-much-of-your-income-should-you-spend-on-housing/

https://www.nomoredebts.org/budgeting-guidelines

https://www.bankrate.com/banking/savings/set-aside-your-spare-change-with-these-money-saving-apps/

https://www.qapital.com/

https://www.longgame.co/

https://www.success.com/19-wise-money-quotes/

https://www.forbes.com/sites/robertberger/2014/04/30/top-100-money-quotes-of-all-time/#69fa5fd44998

www.trahantherapyhouston.com

www.thetrahantherapycenter.com

https://www.amazon.com/10-Ways-Great-Parent-Parenting/dp/097432731X

## MONEY LIES!

1. Only the rich get richer!

**The truth**: People who study money and ways to grow it and implement what they learn consistently and over time grow rich.

2. Only some people are meant to be rich!

**The truth**: Riches come through great effort, purposeful and directed actions done consistently.

3. If you don't know the rich you can't become rich.

**The truth**: You can get to know the rich through books and videos. Eventually, you can meet them.

4. Money is the root of all evil.

**The truth**: When people don't earn and grow money, they often resort to evil deeds to get money. Buy this book for others, share it as a gift.

5. You can borrow your way out of debt.

**The truth**: The very meaning of borrowing is to be indebted to another.

www.ingramcontent.com/pod-product-compliance
Lightning Source LLC
Chambersburg PA
CBHW022050190326
41520CB00008B/768